BIG WORDS FOR LITTLE PEOPLE

Helen Mortimer & Cristina

C000063266

Bravery

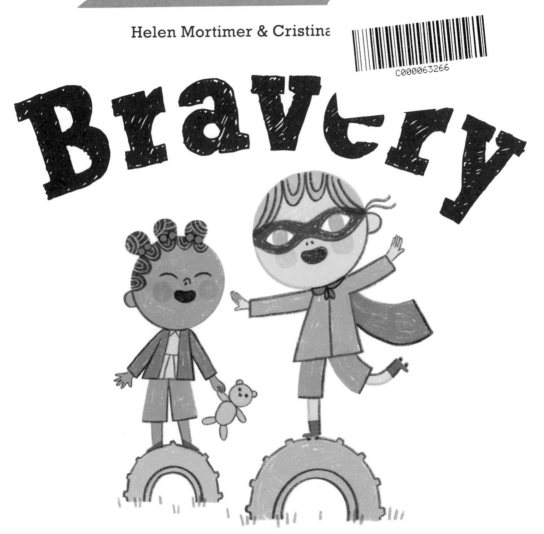

OXFORD
UNIVERSITY PRESS

Try

Being brave can start with trying something for the very first time.

When you believe in yourself it gives you the confidence to take bigger, bolder steps.

Stand up

When you stand up for yourself, or for a friend, you are doing something important.

Dare

Daring is doing things you've never done before, especially when they make you feel anxious.

Strong

If you tell yourself you
are strong it can help you
cope with difficult things.

I am
strong.

You can be a hero!

Calmness

Staying calm makes it easier
to face the things that make us
fearful and nervous.

Different

Never be afraid of being different.

Just focus on what makes you you.

Help each other

Sometimes it is easier to
take on a challenge with
a friend.

Owning up

Owning up and being honest are both kinds of bravery.

Who's got my shoe?

Sometimes telling the truth can be the bravest thing you do.

Lead

It's brave to lead the way, but it's brave to follow, too!

Speaking up

With spirit and a heart full of courage,
you can always make a difference.

Bravery

There are so many ways to be brave.

Be strong. Be confident.
Believe.

Ten ideas for getting the most from this book

1 Take your time. Sharing a book gives you a precious chance to experience something together and provides so many things to talk about.

2 This book is all about what it means to be brave. Talk about ways to be brave and the bravest thing you've done (or seen someone else do) today.

3 It's also a book about language. Ask each other what words you would use to describe being brave.

4 The illustrations in this book capture various moments at an adventure playground. We've intentionally not given the children names – so that you can choose your own and perhaps invent something about their personalities. What name would you give the dog?

Button?
Finn?
Lucky?
Spot?

5 Why not suggest what might have happened just before each moment and what might happen next?

6 Try to get inside the heads and hearts of each child. What helps them to feel brave? What stops them from feeling brave?

7 Remember that sometimes there is distance between the words and the pictures. The words might be describing a way to be brave while the picture might show the opposite.

8 By exploring ways to recognize and express how bravery can have a positive impact on everything we do, we hope this book will give children and the adults in their lives the tools they need to make sense of themselves and the world around them.

9 Encourage imagination – describe a piece of crazy equipment that you would invent for an adventure playground. Would you be brave enough to try it? You could draw it, too.

10 You could each choose a favourite bravery word from the book – it will probably be different each time you share the story!

Glossary

challenge – something that is new and exciting but also difficult

confidence – when you have confidence, you are sure you can do something well

courage – when you have courage, you feel able to do something dangerous or difficult even when you are afraid

honest – when you are honest you tell the truth and do not steal or cheat

nervous – if you are nervous you feel afraid and excited because of something you have to do